MERRY CHRISTMAS

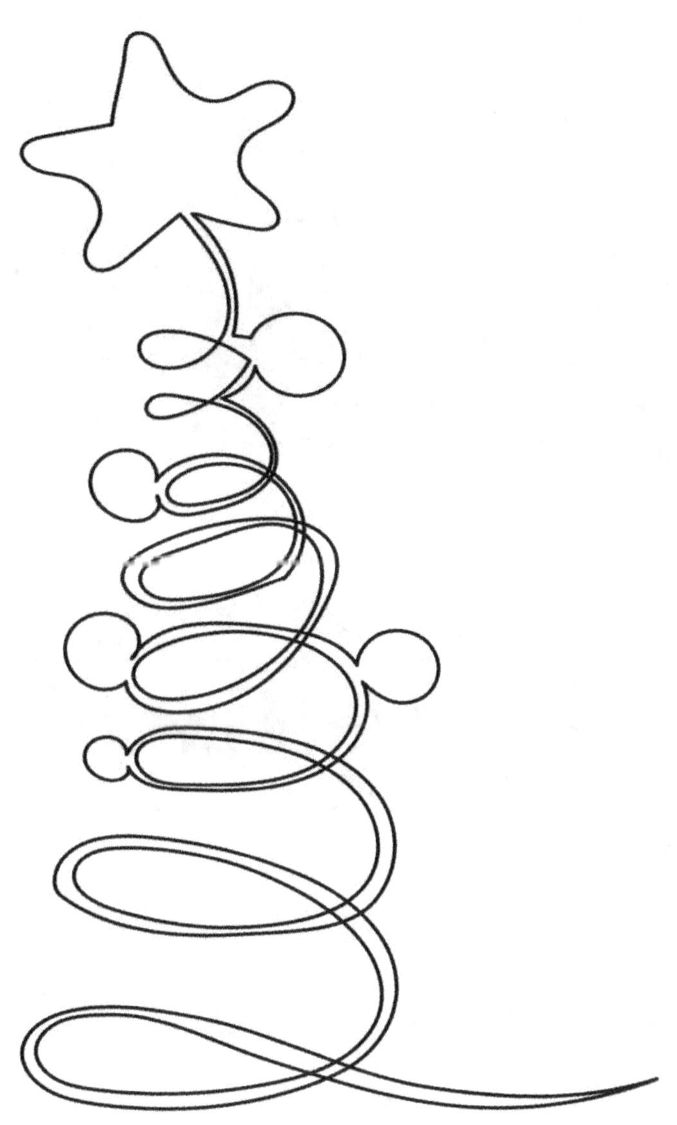

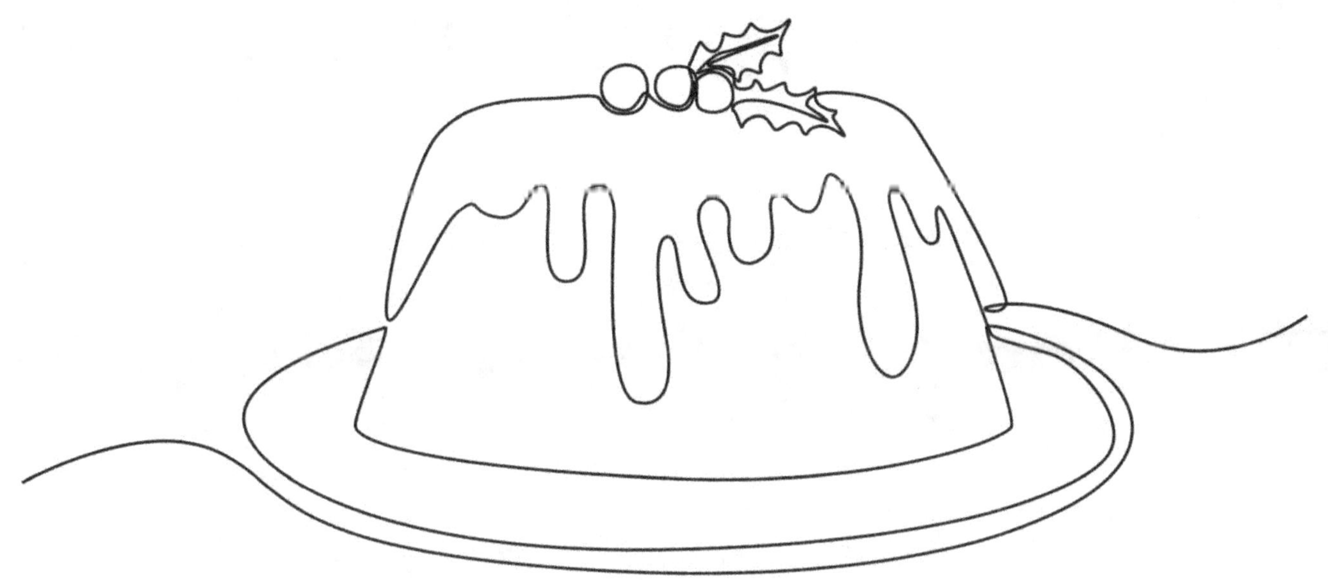

SUE

merry christmas

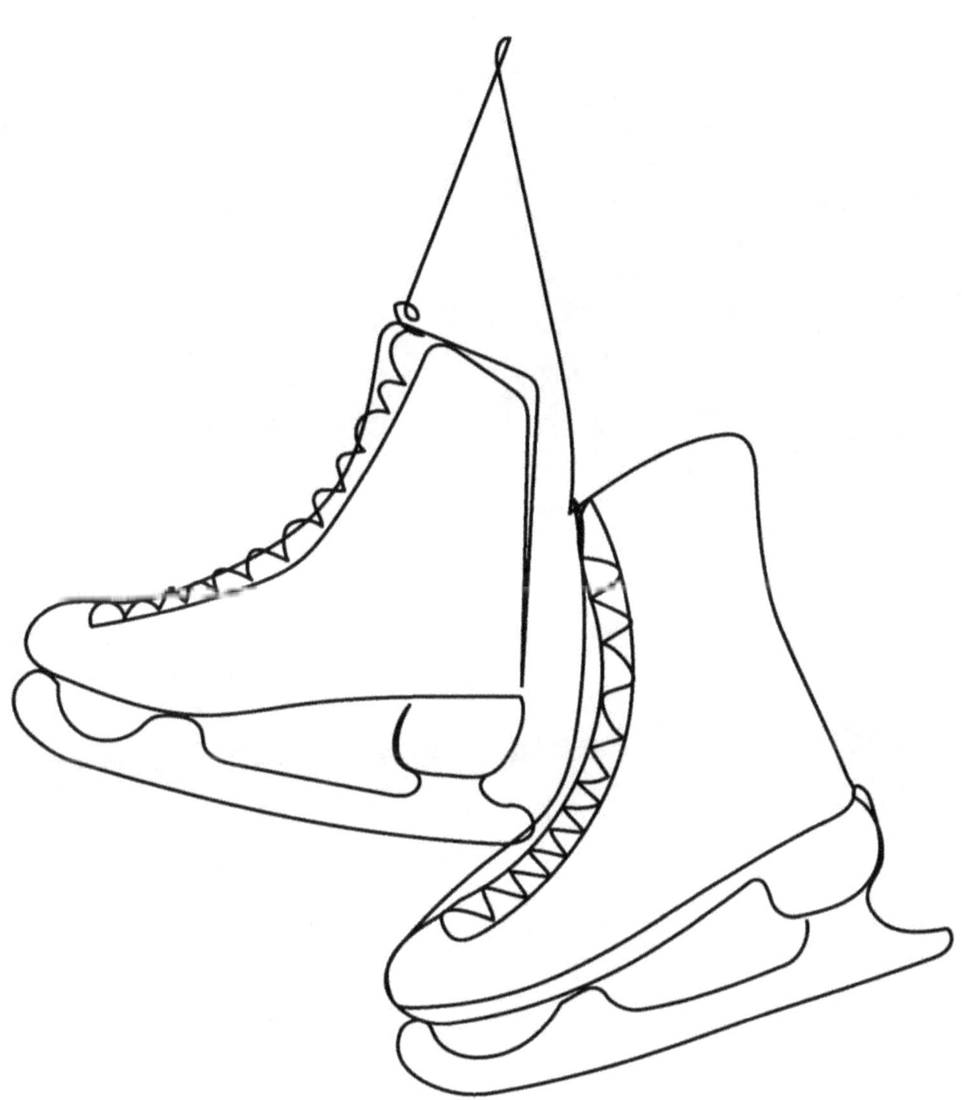

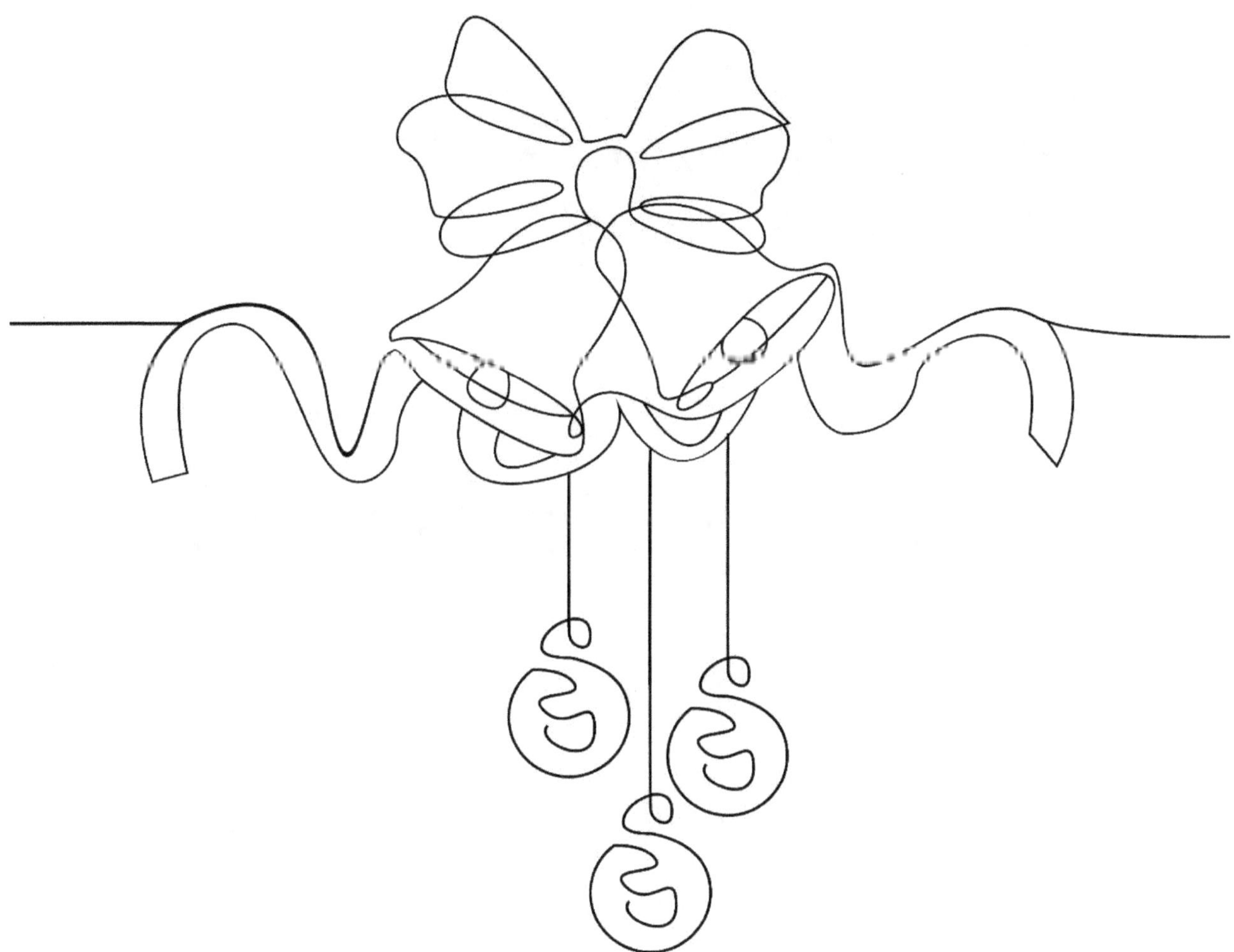

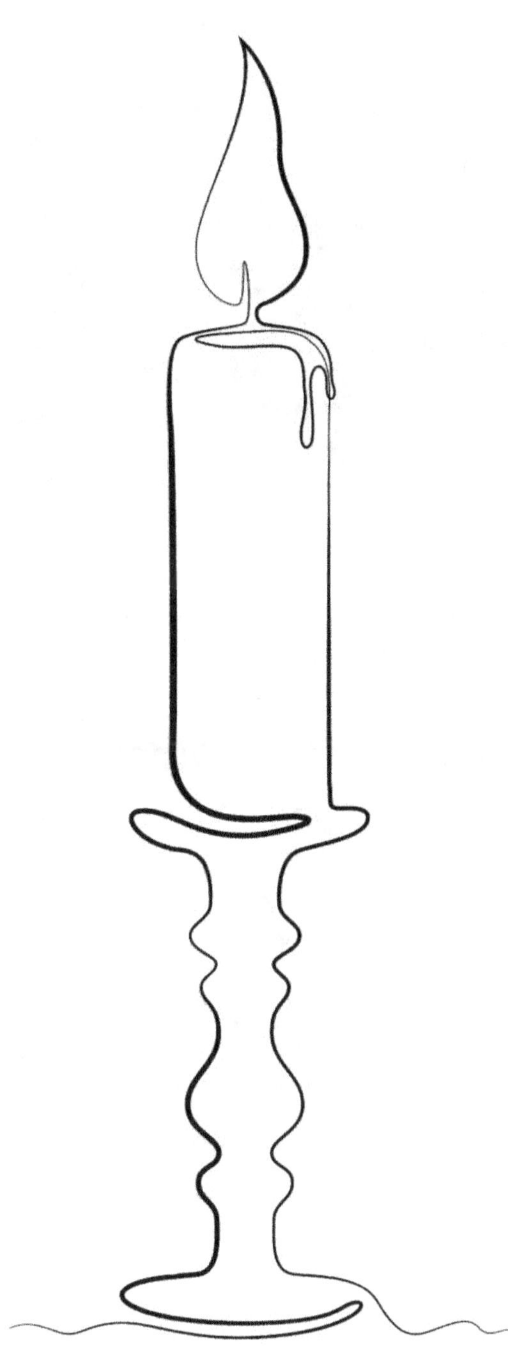

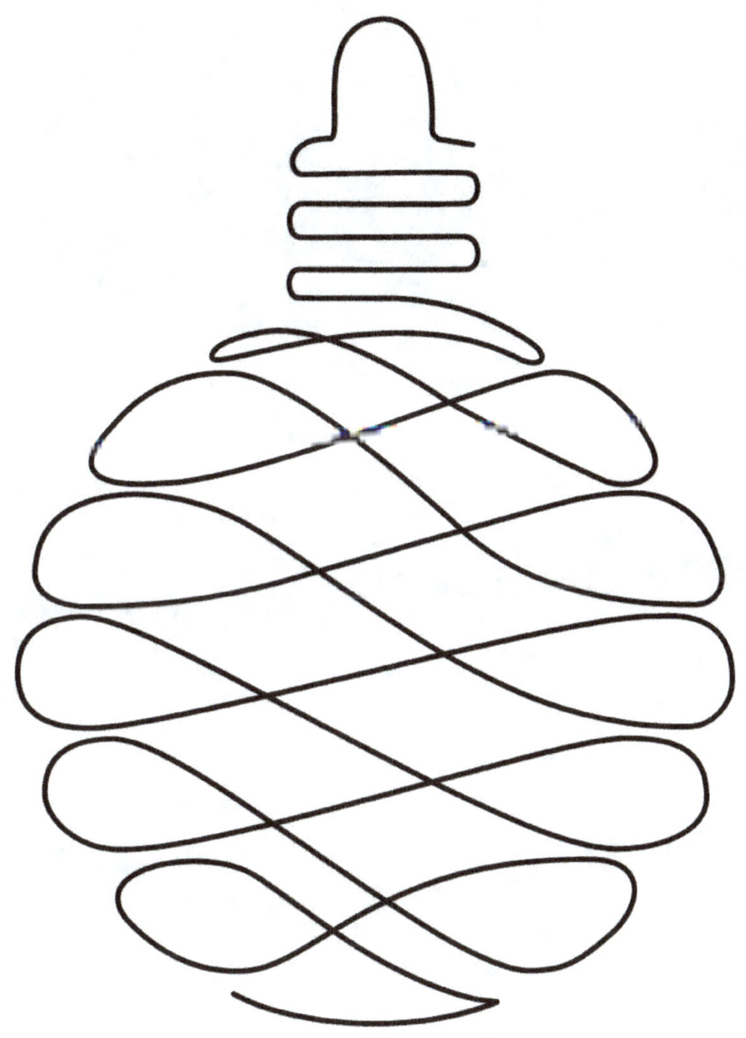

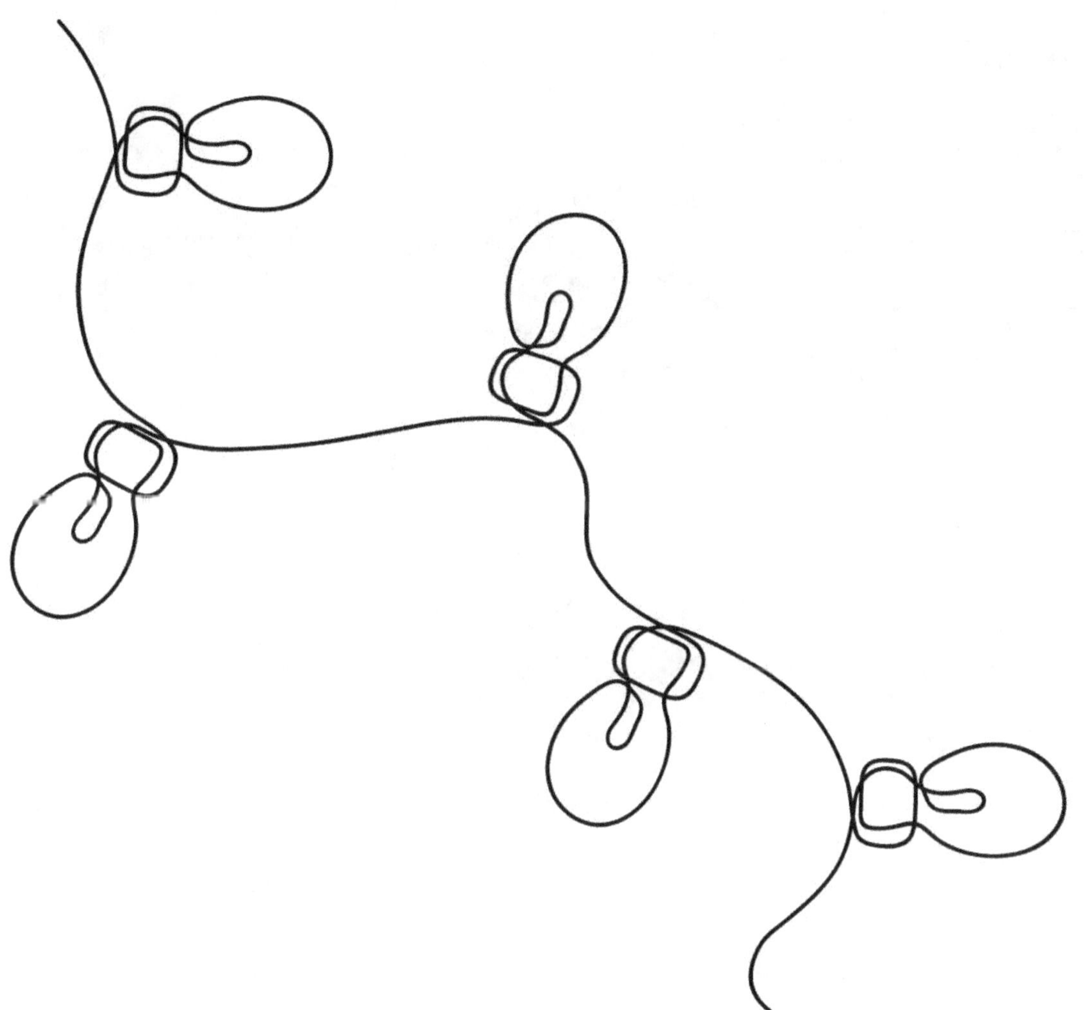

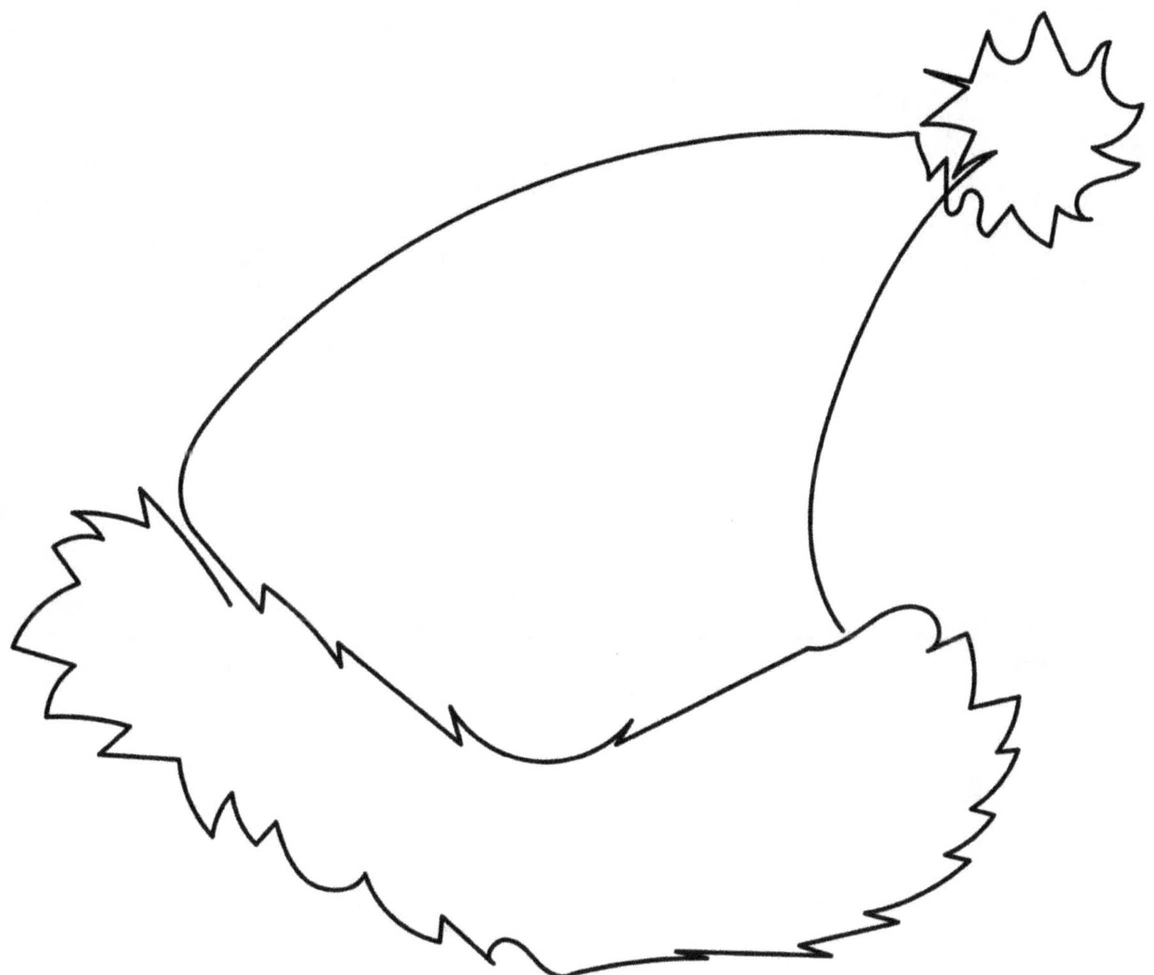

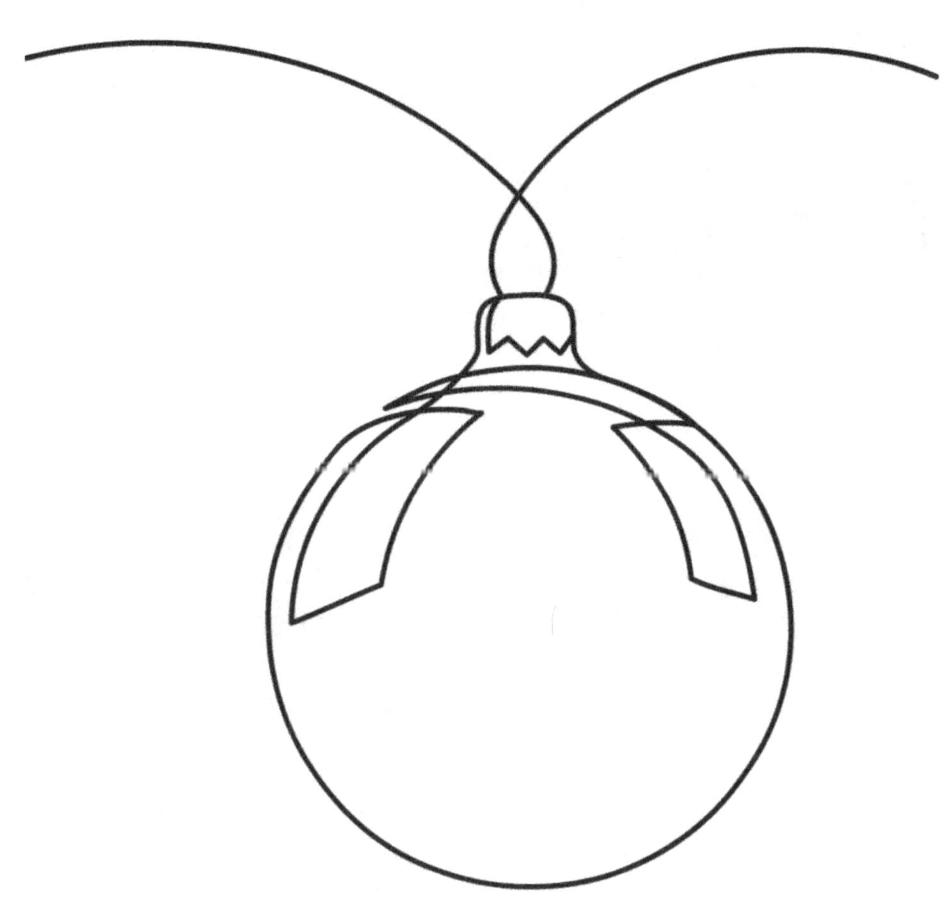

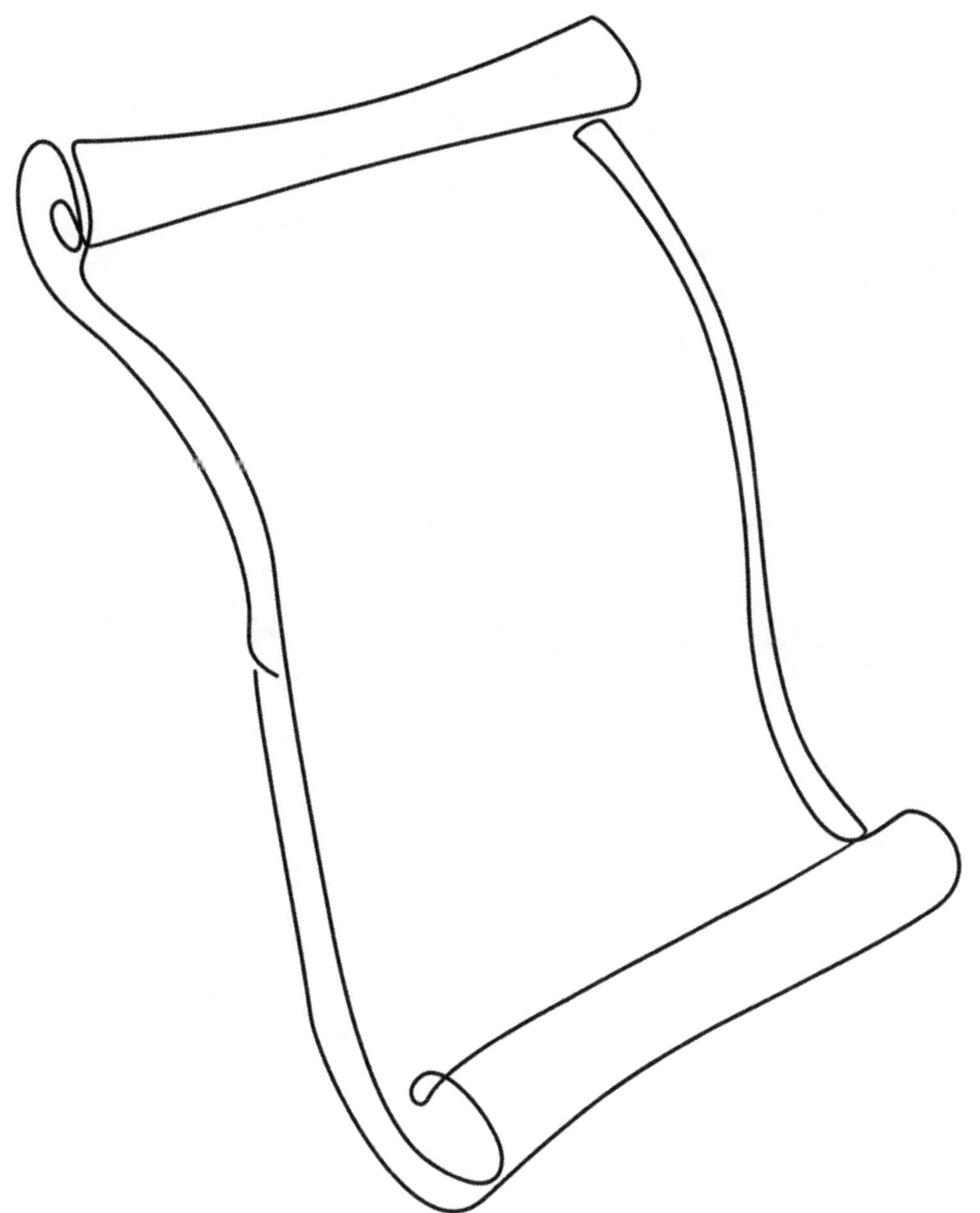